William E. Ninde

A Souvenir of Rome, N.Y.

William E. Ninde

A Souvenir of Rome, N.Y.

ISBN/EAN: 9783744779999

Printed in Europe, USA, Canada, Australia, Japan

Cover: Foto ©ninafisch / pixelio.de

More available books at **www.hansebooks.com**

SOUVENIR OF ROME, N.Y.

A Souvenir of Rome, N. Y.

PUBLISHED BY
WM. E. NINDE
1894

VIEWS ON N. WASHINGTON ST.

LOOKING NORTH

LOOKING SOUTH

FROM THE AMERICAN CORNER

ZION EPISCOPAL CHURCH.

FIRST M.E. CHURCH.

Central N. Y. Institution for the Deaf and Dumb

W.E. MRARGC. ST

N. WASHINGTON St.

St Court St

St George St

Garden St

N.Y.O. & W. Station.

N.Y.C. & H.R.R. Station.

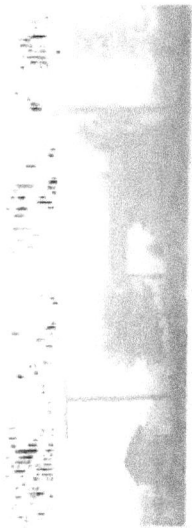

STATE CUSTODIAL ASYLUM.
AND
OLD TOLL GATE.

Birth-place of Albert Barnes

City Hospital

Cemetery and Kingsley Memorial Chapel

The Mohawk, from Floyd Avenue

Selden & Van Wagenen's Planing Mill

County Buildings unfinished

No. 2 Fire Engine House

East Liberty Street

WOOD CREEK
"AT HARLOOSP?"

PELL GEAR WORKS.

FITCH GEAR WORKS.

Newport Iron Mill

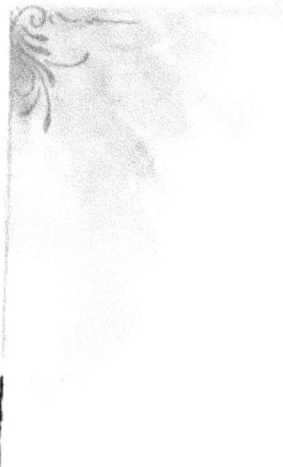

Pam. Boat & Copper Mill

ROME LOCOMOTIVE & MACHINE WORKS.

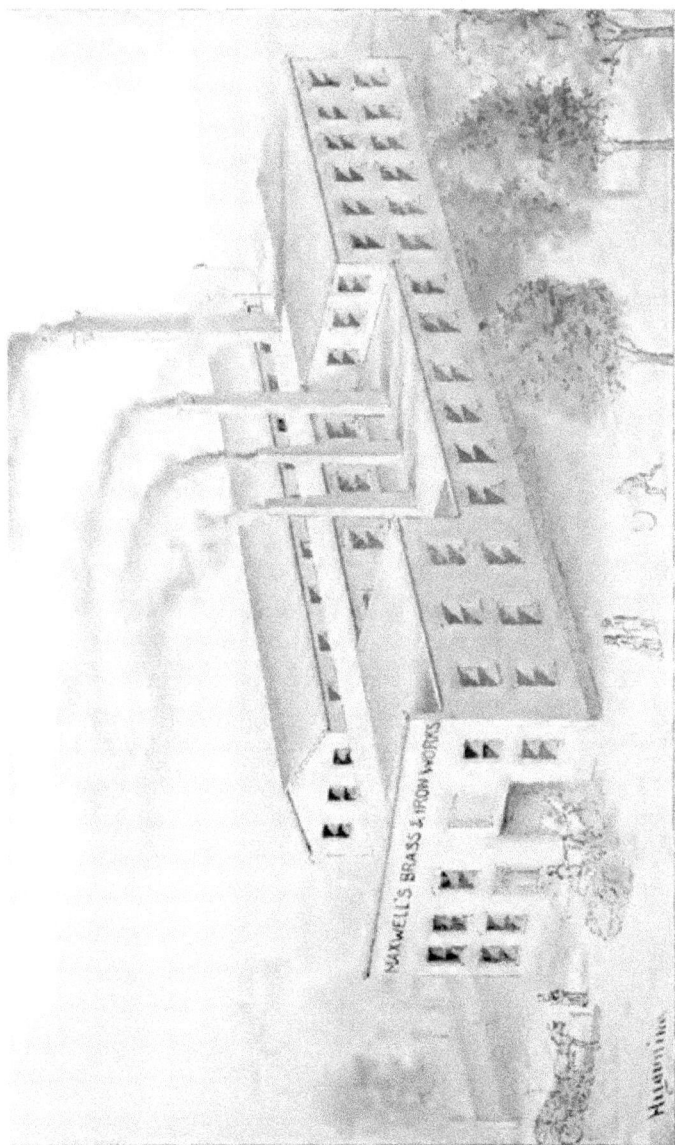

MAXWELL'S BRASS & IRON WORKS

PENFIELD'S SOAP WORKS.

FORT STANWIX CANNING FACTORY.

WILLIAM KNITTING MILLS

COT & CHAIR FACTORY

CARPENTER & DYETT

THE DWELLINGS AND PORTION OF FOUNDATION
OF THE FIRST CO-OPERATIVE CHEESE FACTORY IN
THE WORLD

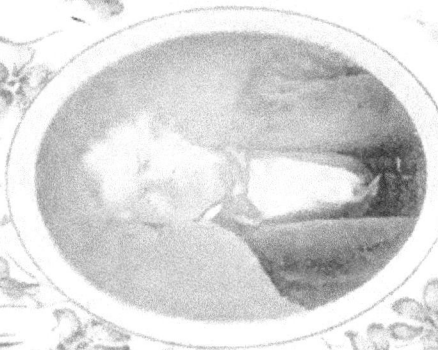

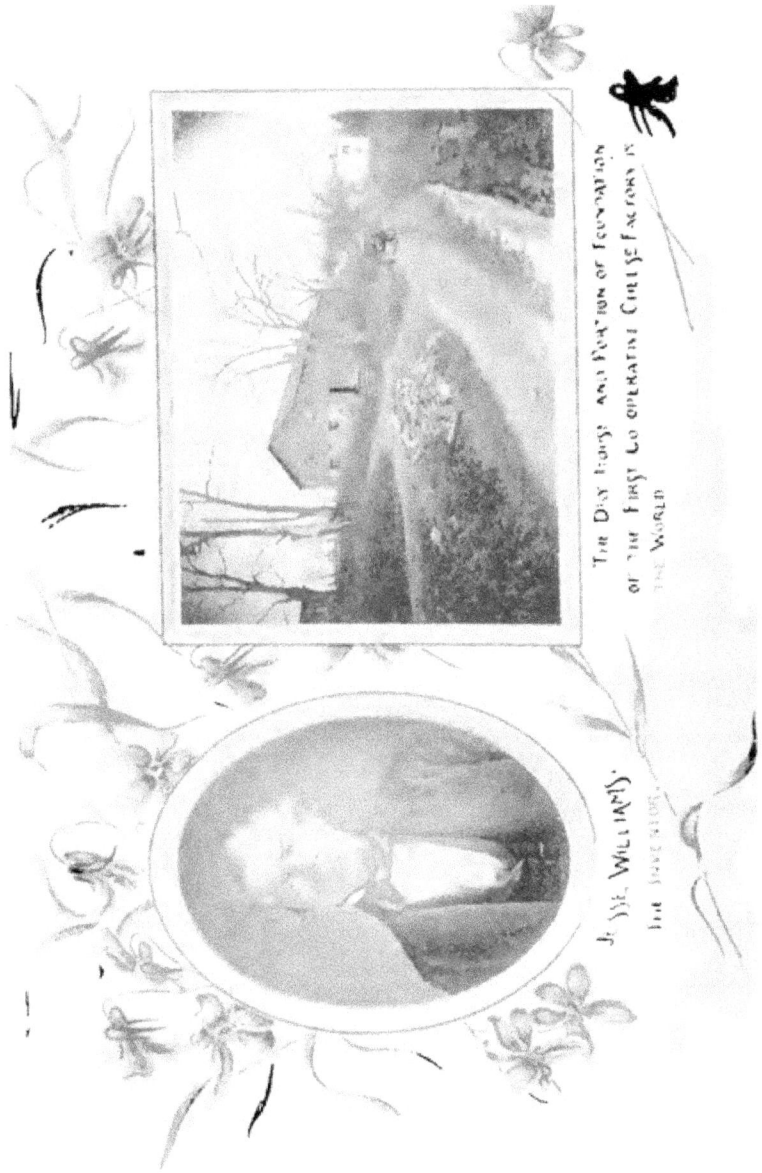

JESSE WILLIAMS,
THE INVENTOR,

CITY LIBRARY. (The [illegible])

OLD ARSENAL HOUSE.

ACADEMY.

CENTRE ST. SCHOOL.

JAY ST. SCHOOL.

CITY HALL
FROM DRAWING

COURT HOUSE & JAIL

ST PETER'S CHURCH.

ST. MARY'S CHURCH.

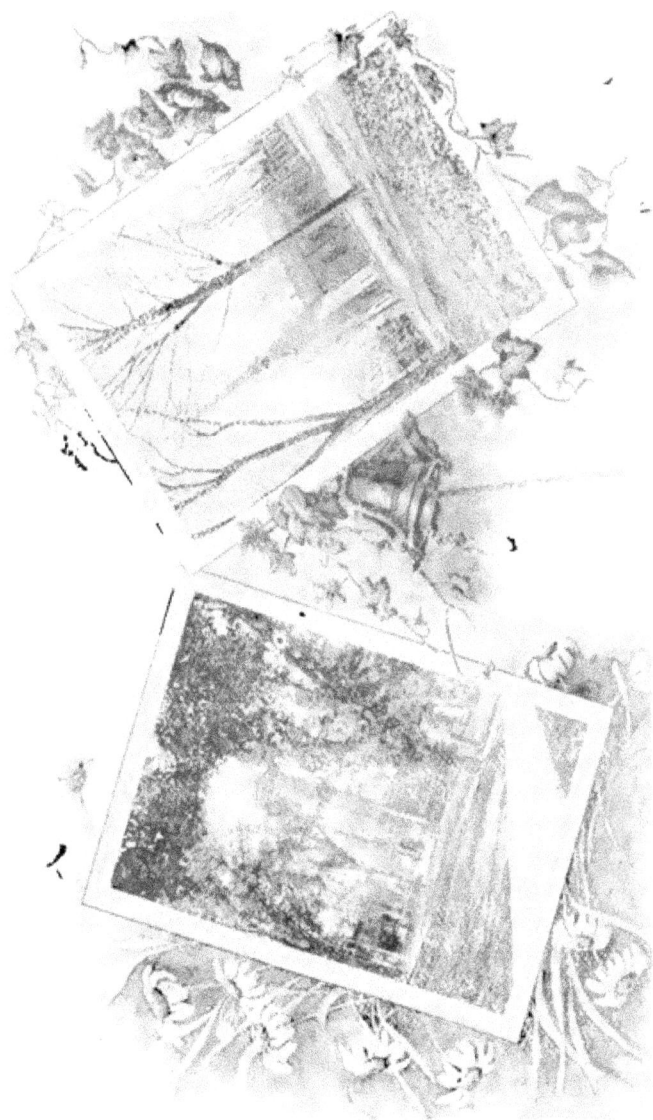

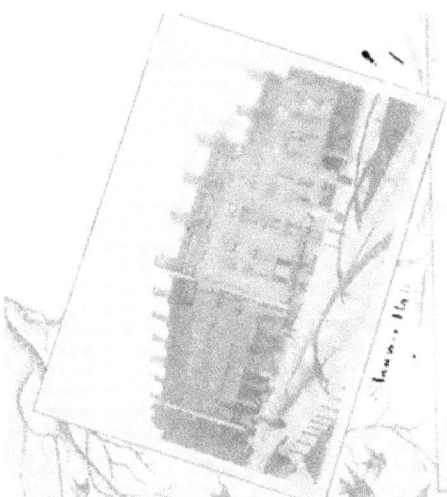

BANKS.

WASHINGTON ST. OPERA HOUSE

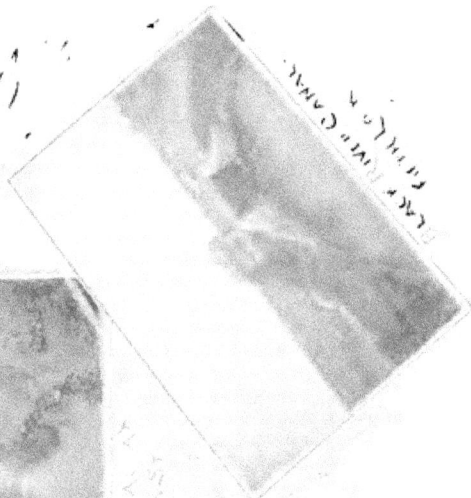

LAKE ERIE CANAL (?)

OLD CANAL AT SUNSET

ERIE CANAL SIXT MILE LEVEL

J. M. Brainerd's Studio

SITE OF FORT BULL.

SITE OF FORT STANWIX.

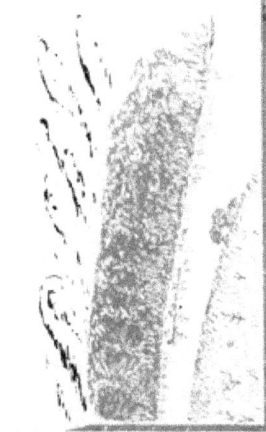

LOOKING WEST

LOOKING EAST

FROM THE AMERICAN CORNER.

Washington St.

CITY WATER WORKS

THE BLOOMFIELD BEACH
ESTATE.

www.ingramcontent.com/pod-product-compliance
Lightning Source LLC
Chambersburg PA
CBHW021426090426
42742CB00009B/1275